318

11·5·79

Living & Dying Gracefully

Herbert N. Conley

PAULIST PRESS
New York/Ramsey/Toronto

Library of Congress
Catalog Card Number: 79-65569

ISBN: 0-8091-0298-6

Published by Paulist Press
Editorial Office: 1865 Broadway, New York, N.Y. 10023
Business Office: 545 Island Road, Ramsey, N.J. 07446

Printed and bound in the
United States of America

C878498

Contents

Dedicated
to
MY WIFE

who in courage,
dignity, and loving support,
has in perfect unity
walked each step of the way

Preface

A few hours ago, I sat in the office of a doctor in Massachusetts General Hospital. During the morning, records of various physical examinations had been delivered to the surgeon. These included proctological exam, biopsy of the colon tumor, liver scan, liver ultrasound and kidney scan. Part of the process had been unpleasant and a little dehumanizing, but all were necessary. Now it was time for evaluation and suggestions for treatment. Would it be surgery, more chemotherapy, radiation or a combination?

The doctor requested that I come into his office alone, leaving my wife outside. This was all the signal that was needed. I had tried to prepare her for what I suspected. The surgeon's face was grave and his concern obvious. To relieve him, I shared that I had correctly read the liver scan machine during the scan process. The radioactive material gave indication that the smaller lobe of the liver was filled with cancer cells. He nodded his head in agreement.

Now, where do we go? With the cancer in two places and one of them (the liver) untreatable, there really wasn't any possibility. Medically, I had come to the end of the road. He suggested that it might be as little as a month or as long as six months, but there would be no prolonged illness. There were suggestions for palliative treatment. Pills could be prescribed for the nausea that would come, and radiation in minimal amounts for pain in the liver area. But the disease would run its course, unimpeded, in a very short period. He stated, again in a sympathetic voice, "You are going to have some rough times ahead. When jaundice comes, you will know there will only be another week or two." We shook hands and I thanked him for his honesty and concern.

On leaving the office, strangely enough, there was some feeling of relief. The worst had finally and decisively happened. There would probably be no surgery or colostomy.

Chances were that the liver tumor would move swifter than the colon tumor. The wearisome chemotherapy was finally a thing of the past. It was now a matter of acceptance, using the last period of time in as meaningful a fashion as possible. The only thing that seemed a bit surrealistic was that excepting for the cancer (which at the moment is not impeding any bodily function) I am in near perfect health. In fact, just a few days before leaving for Massachusetts General, I had played six sets of tennis in one day.

What would you do if you were told that you had ninety days to live? This question was formerly a favorite at intimate parties, along with "What would you do if you inherited a million dollars?" It was all theorizing about the impossible and the bizarre. But a generation is now awakening to the reality of the first question. That which I am facing is unfortunately not unique to many thousands of persons each year.

But more importantly, American society is beginning to accept the fact that dying and death are not abnormal interruptions in the developing process of life, but are actually the climax toward which all life moves. A few years ago it was stated that in the Victorian period, man talked of death but discussion of sex was taboo. In the present period, man has talked about sex beyond satiation, but sought to ignore death as a nonreality. Such can no longer be said.

Bookstores are filled with books by Dr. Kübler-Ross, the psychiatrist who has become the leading authority on death and dying. One of the significant comedians of our day, Woody Allen, has made a career talking about his fear of death. He has endeared himself to man with such quips as "I don't want to achieve immortality by the works I do. I want to achieve it by not dying." And, "I'm not afraid of death, I just don't want to be there when it happens." Whether it is serious emotional drama such as *Love Story* or slapstick comedy, *The End*, more and more movies have death as the plot catalyst. The book *Life After Life*, describing the experiences of those who have been clinically pronounced dead and have been restored, is a national best seller. This has been the subject on many TV talk shows.

Man is struggling to face the ultimate experience. He can think of it theoretically, and even relate it to those he knows. But when he applies the possibility to himself or those closest to him, all manner of fears and anxieties begin to surface. Perhaps the worst

How could it have happened? This is one of the first questions asked, especially if the trigger for the experience is cancer. What caused it? What did I eat that I shouldn't have? What has been wrong in my life style? Even as this is being written the newscaster announces that the government has discovered a cancer producing ingredient in most patent medicine sleeping tablets. It appears that there is almost nothing we ingest that isn't potentially cancer producing. The same is true with our exposure to the sun, to certain kinds of dust, to special rays in medicine and industry, and even to daily stress. The American Cancer Society tells us that one out of every four Americans now living will experience cancer in some form. While over fifty percent will recover, this is little consolation. There is no gold-plated assurance that you will be on the winning side.

If ever man was tempted to be deterministic and say, "It will either happen to me or it won't", this is the time. But this misses the point entirely. The disease may be escapable, but death isn't. You see, our real problem is with death, not with the disease. And since death is inevitable, the serious question is "How am I going to react to dying?" What determines and produces our reaction, as to

of the hobgoblins is the fact of his or her own nonexistence. As a child of ten I was told that a woman friend of the family was seriously ill with cancer. This concerned me, as I had not had contact with death relating to anyone I knew. However, the problem from a child's point of view seemed easily solvable. I simply prayed for her healing every night and gave it no more thought. This ritual went on for weeks. Then came word through my parents that she had experienced death. My trauma was complete and the world came apart. Prayer doesn't work. God doesn't care. And finally, what had happened to the family friend? She was obviously gone forever.

A few nights later, the thought came overpoweringly that this was going to happen to me. My childish mind could not handle the possibility that some day I might not exist and would never exist again. The night was long as a frightened little boy huddled in a bed and wished that dawn would come. At some time, whether young or old, a similar experience occurs to each one. Usually, our response is suppression. The door is quickly locked. How difficult as a rational adult, to open that door, to accept the pain and fear, and to begin to accept life as it is.

This little book of final meditation, in the

midst of the experience, is dedicated to and written for all others who are presently walking a similar path.

Death—
How We Respond

From the time of my own surgery for cancer, I discovered something wondrous had happened. I had instant entree to other cancer patients. When I could say "Brother patient", there seemed to be trust and communication almost automatically. Again, my words were not theory and they had a new validity, that which can only come through experience. In the past year, a major portion of my time has been spent with those diagnosed as having cancer. We have shared our hopes, our concerns, our psychic and physical pain, as well as victories along the way. It is to these persons that I am addressing this book. It is a continuation of our sharing together our innermost thoughts and feelings.

whether it is positive or negative? It would be simplistic to say that a person will respond to death in exactly the same way that he has responded to life. If he has approached life's experiences with cynicism, fear, hostility and insecurity then we know what to expect in his reaction to approaching death.

But that view is cynical in itself and gives man no credit for the ability to change, to grow, to burst forth, to metamorphosize. As an Episcopal priest I have walked through the death experience with well over a thousand persons. Frequently, I have been closer to them than nurse, doctor or family in the moment of transition. They have responded in so many unique and different ways. For many it has been their finest hour and I have seen the dross fall away and almost a new being emerge. Through it all, it has been difficult not to ask "What caused their response?" What were the occurrences in their life that shaped and molded them for this, their most important date? If we have profiles of the individuals, that which has been poured into them, as well as that which has poured out from them, we have a clue as to how they will act. When Jack Nicklaus birdied the last five holes of a major U.S. tournament to win by a stroke you were not surprised. If you knew his past, that which molded his attitude, and how he had responded to other difficult situations, you knew that it was not only possible but probable. The same judgment could be made of one who folded in the midst of intense pressure. As an example, I would like to share a thumbnail sketch of my own life. These are vignettes of major trauma; the moments where I feel now that I was tested to the depths, or received new input that changed my basic response to life. This will set the stage for an understanding of what I will be saying in the following chapters. How do we learn to live, so that when death is seen to be approaching we are ready to respond fearlessly and gracefully?

My childhood was not dissimilar to many others of the immediate post-Depression period. There were three children in our family who survived infancy, myself and two sisters. I was in the middle. Our parents had little education but strong intelligence and a spirit which sought more than just survival. They believed in themselves and their adequacy. Father was an oilman and that meant the alternation of feast and famine, and complete self-dependence. In material things we were possibly at the top of the middle class. Both parents were hard workers and achievers. All

4

three children have followed the pattern with six college degrees among them and each recognized as a leader in his or her chosen profession.

Looking back over a lifetime of fifty years, a pattern of influence becomes obvious. It is like watching the insertion of the various pieces of the mosaic. As a child I was tremendously shy and had a basic fear of other human beings. Even by the age of high school, if the family had a dinner guest, I would normally absent myself from the table. This led to introspection, some fantasizing, and an inordinate enjoyment of America's favorite indoor sport: self-pity.

Contrasting, however, was the steady example of two parents who, without any advantages, always met life head-on and had confidence that they would come out winners. While I felt personally insecure, I knew that I was loved and that the back-up team was unbeatable.

At twelve years of age, what appeared to be an adolescent diversion became a driving force. I discovered the wonderful world of stage magic. Besides school, the next few years were devoted almost exclusively to reading, planning and countless hours of daily practice before a mirror. Proficiency came and with it the requirement to "go public". To my amazement I found myself before larger and larger groups, until at last I was considered a professional. It was almost schizophrenic. I was still the shy and awkward boy off stage, but one who could feel at ease and at home before an audience of several thousand persons. It appeared that show business in some form would be my profession.

Why magic? Religion had been family habit, perfunctory, and yet essentially meaningless, excepting as a social form. Here was something that talked of mystery, the inner secrets of life, and forces of power beyond man's comprehension. Even though psuedo in character, it suggested that there was more to life than the mundane, the surface characteristics.

At this point came one of the most important life-shaping traumas of my adolescence. Having no brothers, I had found my hero in a brother-in-law. He was handsome, athletically talented, winsome, and a career army officer in the cavalry. Being an only child himself, he had treated me as a cherished little brother and made me feel important.

The Second World War had begun, and he was assigned to the Pacific. His wife, my older sister, with their young child, came back home to live until his return. This had all made little impression on me. At eighteen I was managing a theatre and waiting to be drafted.

Then came the letter. It was in feminine handwriting. The writer, a nurse, explained that my brother-in-law had contracted a jungle disease and was on a ship coming home. He couldn't write because his hands were bandaged, but he was doing very well—considering! I recall feeling some elation that we would see him again. Anticipation began to grow.

One week later Mother met me at the door and she had obviously been crying. I don't believe that I had ever seen her cry. She said, with a tone of helplessness, "Clark is dead."

It was absolutely unreal. A telegram came saying that he had died aboard ship. Could it be a mistake? Was there any way to turn the clock back and undo it? I recall fleeing the house. There were tears and screaming rage. It was totally unacceptable. Life isn't fair. It is all irrational nonsense. Who in his right mind would build a beautiful home and just as it was finished put a torch to it? Who would paint a magnificent canvas and then slash it to oblivion before the paint was dry? In effect, this is what had happened with the death of my friend.

For a few months I took pride in a quiet but militant atheism. The world must awaken to the meaninglessness, the psychotic frivolity of life itself. As if to assure myself, I began to study religion in general and Christianity in particular. There was a condescending note of pity for superstitious people. As the study progressed and I became exposed to some of the brightest and noblest minds of all ages, a subtle transformation took place. Life was seen and experienced in new dimensions and much larger perspective.

Saul Alinsky taught that crisis is never good or bad. It simply means that major change is about to take place. Our response to crisis determines its moral value. My exposure to the day by day life of Jesus was a converting experience. His response to each opportunity and confrontation revealed meaning and purpose. Here was that reality behind the superficial that I had sought for so long. Shortly, I was back at the university studying as a pre-theological student. One of my first actions was to give away a vast storage of magic equipment. Having discovered the real, the ersatz had no allure.

As the result of the death of a loved one, my whole life had been reoriented, changed in its inner structure as well as outward observance.

My career as an ordained clergyman spanned three decades and six congregations. The work was basically three-sided. There was the administrative side. It consisted mostly of planning, training leadership and development of organization and program. In five of my last six churches, there was at least one major building program while I was there. And in the last two churches, including my seven years as Dean of the Cathedral in Honolulu, I was a worker-priest. This means that I also was heavily involved in responsibilities in the business world.

A second phase of the ministry is theological and theoretical. Day in and out I taught the doctrines of the historic Christian faith and sought to experience them in my life. There was often frustration because of the tremendous gap between the theory and man's own personal experience of truth. Sometimes these made little contact.

The most significant aspect was the pastoral and personal side. Here I lived with my people on almost a family basis. With them I faced the tragedies, the injustices, and the pain that so frequently came. Together we wrestled with sickness, suffering and death. So much that assaults the sensibilities of man is not due to man's failure or innate sinfulness. At times the very fact of the tribulations presents problems in reconciliation with the Christian doctrines of the goodness of God and His omnipotence. The New Testament stresses the problem, especially in the life of Jesus. I was in constant contact with death. There was death from disease, suicide and accident. When disease was the cause, there was time to be with the parishioner daily, to talk it through and experience it until the final moment of separation from a tired or distorted body. While I was seeking to bring faith, warmth, understanding and hope, my own insight and view of the death experience was being radically altered. Finally, I could understand Paul's statement: "O death, where is thy sting? O grave, where is thy victory? Thanks be to God who giveth us the victory in Jesus Christ". This was not pollyanna-ish hiding behind doctrine or vain hope. Paul had experienced truth on a level that transcended this very temporal existence. He was expressing knowledge rather than belief.

In these years, the outward profile of my life was not that much different from the average executive. The day usually began about 5:00 A.M. and continued to exhaustion late at night. Physically, my body was kept in excellent condition. No smoking, and little alcohol. Weight was maintained according to medical recommendations. There were six miles of jogging, three times a week, plus tennis. Excellent health was obvious.

Then at fifty-one, the telltale signs of colon cancer appeared. The bishop, my administrative superior, had died of colon cancer the year before. I remarked to myself that it was mathematically impossible for the two top officers of any organization to be struck down by the same disease within twelve months. So, the symptoms were ignored for almost two months. Finally, a visit to the family internist for a diagnosis without examination: that my illness was just a matter of emotional pressure and pills were prescribed to take care of everything. The fault was more mine than the doctor's for not insisting on a proctological examination. The symptoms persisted and so a visit was made to another internist. Tests were run immediately and the tumor discovered. Within four days I was in for six hours of surgery.

Due to the skill of the surgeon, a colostomy was not required. The surgical report looked good; the tumor was limited, well-defined, and evidently not expanded beyond its own boundaries. There would still be several days' wait for the lab report. On the third day of surgical recovery, the only doctor to enter my room was the cancer specialist and I knew instantly. My situation was medically terminal.

Microscopic examination indicated that the tumor had broken into the lymph glands and blood vessels. Positive nodes were found outside the tumor. The oncologist was very honest. "After about a month, we will try chemotherapy to cool things off. With some, the drug does fairly well, with others it slows it down a bit, and with some it has no effect." Circumstances would indicate that I was in the latter category.

Lying immobile in a hospital bed for the next two days, there were long hours to contemplate what it all meant. Death would be experienced within a few months. My mind flooded with uncontrolled thoughts. The pain-killing drugs confused the issue further by limiting my mind's ability to function. I felt no concern about the disease, about the experience of death, about the end of personal existence here. But there was a devastating sense of failure to meet responsibilities. What

I had hoped to do at the Cathedral would not be done. A business that was still in the infancy period would be left to flounder. Deepest depression came from my economic situation. There was very little money for the family. As a husband and father who had been financially responsible all the years, death wouldn't relieve that responsibility. My mind worked with insurance, house equity, pitiful church pension fund. But the figures came out woefully short.

Suddenly my temperature shot to a hundred and four. From one in the afternoon until three A.M. there was a constant flurry of activity at my bedside. Chills, convulsions, icepacking, were the order of the day. The fever left as quickly as it had come. The culprit had been intense, all consuming anger. I had met my match. The situation was totally out of my control. For the moment, I felt myself to be the victim of the disease, and those I loved would be hurt and vandalized.

In the next few days, the planning and ministry of a sensitive and loving business partner erased my greatest concern. The family could and would continue to receive regular income from the business and not fall to dependent status. With my mind freed, an outline of those things to be completed and accomplished in the months remaining was written. During the past eleven months about eighty percent of the list has been fulfilled. Now I have a feeling of peace and thankfulness. The rapidly approaching death experience is neither threatening nor frightening. It is accepted as a normal part of the life process. What have I learned in these years which brings about this response to the Ultimate Experience?

Getting a Grasp
on Reality

What is reality to you? An alarm clock going off in the morning, a new car, Ethan Allen furniture, the sun, moon and stars. Most think of reality as the tangible world beyond us. Of course there is an objective reality "out there." But, is that actually reality to you? Imagine a mother weeping over her child. What is the reality of the situation? Objectively, we could receive a biochemical report on bodily function. Would that sum up the reality of the experience? Hardly. The physical is a manifestation of something far more profound. The reality to the mother is the anguish, pain and heartbreak which is being expressed through the body. Obviously, there is a reality beyond the senses of man.

Let's take a step further. Notice that we asked, "What is reality to you?" Reality to you is what you experience. All else is theory. We surround, confuse and limit ourselves by theory, pretending that it is reality. Ninety-three percent of all Americans believe that God exists. It is doubtful that He is complimented by this Gallup report. Only a tiny percent live day by day as if it is a fact. For those few it is experiential reality. For the others, it is theory and does not have meaning nor does it alter the course of their existence. For years I listened to a friend who was fervent on civil rights and racial equality. He could destroy any party within an hour and distribute guilt in a flagrant fashion. One day I asked him how many black people he knew as personal friends, and how many had been guests in his home in the past year. It was all theory, finding a sense of inner righteousness by taking a strong moral stand. But there was no personal reality to him in the issue.

Reality to you is the inner world of your experience, from a toothache, to holding hands, to a banana split enjoyed, to a raise in salary, to a lost ball game in which you have emotionally invested. This now leads us into a second fact about reality to you. It is the other side of the coin. Reality is your relationship to that objective world outside you. Take a painted wall. Do you realize that the color is not in the wall? The paint causes the light to reflect off of the wall in a certain way. The color is within your eye as the light strikes it. The principle is easily observed in the clear diamond as it takes on all the colors of the rainbow. The color is produced in the relationship of the eye to the light being reflected off the wall.

What happens in the objective world outside us is not all that significant. But how we respond and relate to it and feel about it is enormously important, for this is our reality. Remember the last gloomy day. You were down on everything and everybody and life wasn't very pleasant. Then in the midst of the day something delightful and unexpected happened. It may have been the receiving of good news. Suddenly, the whole day was changed. You were smiling and enjoying those around you. Basically, the general circumstances around you had not changed. But the whole world had changed as far as you were concerned. The difference was that you had changed your relationship to the externals of the world. When you were gloomy, in your view, that was reality. But it was also reality to you when you became elated.

If you have followed our discussion and generally agreed up to this point, you are in trouble. The next and logical conclusion is that it really doesn't matter that much what the exterior facts or problems are. Reality is how I relate to them, and I can do something about that. Tens of thousands of lives have been changed by a single sentence, uttered by a wise man, "If you want to change your life, change your attitude." He was simply suggesting that within you there are the tools to change your experience of and your relationship to those events taking place around you. And in the process you may even change the events.

What does all this have to do with your doctor's statement that you have cancer and it may be beyond medical assistance? As I sit and write to you, there are two tumors within me growing at an ever increasing rate. I have already experienced sensitivity and slight discomfort in both areas. Thus it is reality to me and not theory. The only question is, "Am I to be swallowed up in this reality, allow it to overwhelm me, to dominate every nook and cranny of my existence? Are the days that remain to be blackened and made nightmarish?" Hardly! You see, it is but one reality out of many in my life. Today, I am having the job of sharing with you. This evening I will join with my doctor and his wife for a lovely dinner at the country club. This week I will be returning to Hawaii to put the finishing touches on a contemporary house that we are building, to complete the fiscal year of a company of which I am president and to plan for its continued expansion, and to provide support and assistance for my bishop and the diocese. All of these are gracious, constructive realities. I am surrounded by a devoted family, loving friends, and concerned medical personnel. These are tremendously significant realities in my life. For me, the experience of the Presence of God, and His loving nature, is the ultimate Reality.

Without ignoring the serious and altering nature of the reality of cancer, it is still a rather minor reality in the structure of life and should be given no more attention or concern than it is due. It will occupy the spotlight for a few brief weeks before the experience of death, but until then it is simply a harassing inconvenience. You have the power within you to select the priority of your realities. Why not major in the best?

Your Mind as
the Central Keyboard

Napoleon Hill astounded a segment of our society with his book *Think and Grow Rich*. While not all his readers have found themselves shoulder to shoulder with the Rockefellers and the Morgans, those who have followed his counsel to "think" have discovered an expansive new world. Man tends to go through life as a reactor. His brain, when used, is dedicated to problem solving. The negative happens and he tries to reason as to what to do about it. The thought that he can be the actor, the prime force as a positive factor to which all else reacts, never occurs.

To oversimplify, the brain works in two basic ways. It feeds into the memory computer the experiences that are considered significant. Later it decides what material is to be recalled and played on the screen of man's emotions. Its computer program for selection and recall is constructed in the years of infancy and pre-adolescence by parents, relatives, playmates and teachers.

Too often this programming is centered in anxiety, fear, self-defeat and self-pity. Any negative experience immediately conjures up, from the conscious and unconscious, the emotion of all similar experiences of the past. This inundates us and literally paralyzes our ability to handle the situation positively and creatively. Alcoholics Anonymous has a saying "There is no situation so bad, so threatening, so destructive, that a drink can't make it worse." Most of us don't need that drink to play the game. We have powers of meditation that would put a guru to shame—and we use them, for the most part, for negative reflection. I have contemplated writing a book on America's favorite indoor sport entitled *How To Maintain Depression When All Is Going Well.*

But this marvelous instrument, the human mind, was meant to give you an enormous say in regard to your destiny. By deliberately choosing what goes in and basically what is recalled, life can be turned around. Of course, there is no absolute control, nor am I suggesting suppression. But we must begin to exercise our choices. When we are told that we have cancer, mentally it is like opening Pandora's box of fears. Every anxiety-laden emotion which we have stored away rises to the surface and grips the being. There is fear of the medical treatment, fear of pain, fear of the body becoming ugly, and the list continues on without end. These are involuntary responses but totally real.

At this point the mind has a heavy job. The basic question is whether the emotions are going to control the mind or the mind is going to control the emotions. Each one of the fears will have to be addressed as objectively as possible to see what is fact and what is myth. Information can be secured from the doctor, clergy, library and other sources. There will still be a normal residue of anxiety that remains, once we have sifted through our negative fantasies.

The next principle is never to let the negative thought or the poisonous emotion linger. Deal with it. Accept its potential message. Get it in proper perspective. Then replace it with that which is quite positive or pleasurable. Treat life as normal and it will be. Of course this is an act of discipline and will.

The second secret is that the mind must

turn from the thought of self to others. Introspection and contemplation of the disease will throw you into the self-pity syndrome. The central redemptive principle in A.A. is that there is no recovery until the alcoholic moves outside himself and starts doing things for others. When I was a parish priest, and began to feel a bit of despondency, I would flee to the nearest hospital for an afternoon of visiting. It worked like magic. By the time the visits were over, the world had righted. It wasn't a matter of feeling better off than those less fortunate. The principle is simply that I cannot think of my problems and be thinking of someone else at the same time. So, choosing to think of others and to relate to them, I had broken the think chain of minor depression.

Finally, cultivate the practice of being thankful. In thirty years of counseling others, I can seldom recall an individual burdened by oppressive anxiety who had the personal habit of thanksgiving. Habitual thanksgiving seems to automatically keep all the priorities in right order. All during the day so many nice little things are happening from finding a lost key, to a deep blue sky and bright sun, to another driver letting you cross lanes, to imbibing of your favorite dessert. Cancer doesn't stop any of these things from happening. In fact, you will discover that as people are aware of what you are facing, there will be almost an explosion of things for which to give thanks. Thanksgiving can reconstruct your preoccupation with disease. "As a man thinketh in his heart, so is he." The mind is your answer.

Charlatans, Quacks, and Other Friends

After one has stabilized a bit from the original diagnosis, hope comes from complete recovery. Somehow, someway, we desperately desire that all things be back as they were. Well, for approximately fifty percent of those pronounced ill with cancer, there will be complete recovery. Part will be due to early discovery, and the rest due to skillful surgery, or chemical treatment, especially with leukemia and Hodgkin's disease. This percentage will continue to increase as the scientific breakthroughs come. The future is very promising. Still for hundreds of thousands a year, medical science has to say "Sorry, there is basically nothing more that we can do." The mind and spirit simply can't accept the hopelessness of that position. The individual will desperately look for that special treatment, the miracle of miracles; or that he or she will be the one in a hundred where the body suddenly attacks the cancer. After eight and a half years of struggle, and many surgeries, and devastating chemotherapy, Hubert Humphrey could say "I haven't given up. I believe in miracles." And we all understood and cheered this brave man.

The person with cancer, from the first, is going to be besieged by stories, written and oral, about remission of the disease. The spectrum will span from Lourdes, to a neighbor's grandmother who used a special herb in her tea. The remissions are probably true, though some are the result of imagination or misdiagnosis. As a priest, I have shared with my physician friends in some very moving experiences of remission.

In one parish there was an attractive six-year-old girl. She had, with diligent assistance from her parents, overcome deafness. She was able to lip-read with rare skill. The parents noticed some change in behavior and the right eyelid began to droop. Finally it was closed and swollen. Tests indicated a brain tumor. The surgeon, who was a personal friend of the family, came out of surgery with the tears flowing. There was a tumor and it was obviously malignant. He had removed as much as he could, which would bring temporary relief. But the skull was also perforated from the disease. The time would be quite short. The child today is a grown young lady, in perfect health. Of course, there were prayers and much faith surrounding the child, as there is in almost every case of critical illness. The body destroyed the disease and repaired the damage. Someday with the help of science, this may be the norm, rather than the unbelievably rare exception.

In another parish I was introduced to a plucky young woman, divorced and with child. Cancer had been discovered in her arm and shoulder. She was sent to the City of Hope on the West Coast. When they told her it was too extensive and they could do nothing, she insisted that they take off the arm and shoulder which they did. Within nine months her local doctor told me that x-rays revealed that her lungs were filled with cancerous tumors. I sought to begin to prepare her for the experience that was coming. Three months later, I received a call from the doctor. He was in a state of excitement and wondered if I could come to his office immediately. Upon arrival, he showed me the original x-rays, clearly revealing the tumors. Then we looked at the x-rays of that morning. They were as clear as those of a new-born child. The body had eradicated the disease. In the next two years, she married a wonderful and responsible man. He adopted her daughter and she had, for the first time, a beautiful life. Then the cancer returned and she was gone in a short period. Remissions are there, but they are the very rare exception. As science continues its massive research into the immunological system, we will discover eventually all the resources necessary, within the individual, to rout cancer. The capacity is there at the present time. But our chemical security police force tends to ignore what is happening, and fails to recognize the cancer as a foreign element. If remission is to be yours, it will come, and simply give thanks for the opportunity of the extended time.

Prepare, however, for your mind to be assaulted in oral and written form, by those who have the magical formula which will save you. Coupled with man's innate desire to be saved, is the guilt that says "What if I ignore it, and it really would have worked?" The amateur practitioners have no doubts. I have been guaranteed physical salvation if I will regulate my protein intake, balanced with the absorption of artificial pancreas enzymes.

Then there was the cure that began each day with a coffee enema! Two of the movements insisted that if you would send a urine specimen, they could tell you exactly where the cancer is located as well as all pre-cancerous cells in the body. The cures are as limitless as the imagination of man. Many of them are in good faith and couched in scholarly language.

Some are not totally without truth. Years ago, with parishioners, I drove to a poor area of Amarillo, Texas. We pulled up in front of a small, white frame house. In the driveway were two brand new Cadillacs (his and hers). The owner traded cars every six months. He only practiced his trade of healing sixteen days of each month. The rest of the time was spent relaxing. His per case fee was approximately $1,500 in today's money value. It was a one time, flat charge. The drugs he dispensed were additional. Throughout the day, the waiting room was filled with men, women, and children, those who had been diagnosed as hopeless by medical science. After a very personal sales pitch with each one, he sold them a large bottle which contained vitamins in liquid form. The remission rate was probably the same as if they had not seen him. But the vitamins for a short time increased their sense of physical well being.

In the more legitimate areas of those sincerely seeking to find an alternate answer, there is always much truth, whether they are promoting change in diet, overcoming stress, or special chemicals. They are as alchemy was to chemistry, or folk medicine to modern day science.

While many will argue that they keep hope alive within man until the end, what kind of a life is it that must feed on false hope, and cannot face truth? Surely there is more integrity and meaning to life than this. The panaceas help man to avoid and evade the central truths of life, and to ignore the natural forces, the deeper meaning and purpose of existence. It is like locking man in an air conditioned room without windows, so that he will never experience winter or fall. If we can burst through man's fears, and give him sufficient support to stand, he will discover that each phase of life has its own glory and that includes even the death process. Woman made the amazing discovery when she struck in the direction of natural childbirth. She went against human logic and life opened its arms to her. Giving man a chance to prepare for death, to even see it with some honest expectancy and to find that the sick bed has become an altar of Eucharist, of eternal thanksgiving: this is what it is all about.

Exorcising the Myths and Hobgoblins

From the time cancer becomes part of your life, you discover questions begin to play an inordinate part. The first question is "Is it malignant or not?" When that answer is affirmative, we move on to the second question, "Is it contained or has it spread?" If that also is answered affirmatively, then it seems there is only a final question, "How long do I have?" Medical science has no answer to the last one. Those who should have experienced death within weeks have continued for years, while those who seemed best suited to survive have been gone in the twinkling of an eye. The patient is more the key to the answer than is medical science.

There is another question that looms

33

even larger than those we have mentioned. It comes from deep in the boiling caldron of self-pity. "Why me?" "Of all my friends, relatives, business associates, and neighbors, why me?" When the doctor at Massachusetts General had told me that the future had ceased to exist, he said "I'm sure you are asking yourself, 'Why me?' " The truth is, I wasn't. I have had to deal with the question too often in regard to parishioners through the last thirty years.

Asking "Why me?" is perfectly normal and indicates we have fallen into one of society's most precious heresies. It goes like this: though everyone else may die, I shall remain alive. The truth is that nothing has happened to you that isn't going to happen to everyone you know, everyone who now breathes the breath of life. What is happening to you is the common denominator. It has happened to those before you, and it will soon happen to those who follow you. A few months ago I went to visit with a surgeon who had repaired a hernia for me previously. He had just returned from an extended visit in Europe. He was accompanied on the trip by his wife and five of his children. He is a fine man, a hard worker, and a smart business investor. In effect he has everything that Americans prize. The subject got around to my cancer. He inquired as to the particular chemotherapy that I was receiving. As we parted, he said "I'm sincerely sorry for what you are experiencing." While standing waiting for the elevator, there was the temptation to compare the two lives. His life story was building from one success to another, while mine was beginning the last chapter. The day before I left for Massachusetts General, he went into surgery to have a lung removed because of cancer. For each there is a time, but it comes to each one.

Perhaps a more reasonable question is "Why now?" It has taken this long to get my life stabilized. Now I am reaping some of the fruits of the years of labor. It is time to relax and do a few things that there hasn't been time to do before. "Why now?" When would you have chosen for it to happen? None would select the moment when they are in their prime. Would you have preferred it during the early, struggling years, when your responsibilities family-wise were mountainous? Most of us would prefer it before we become doddering and senile. When would you choose? The honest answer is that we would never choose. The choice has to be made for us, and there is never the right time. Give thanks for the faith and strength to face it whenever it comes. C878498

As we contemplate the future from a

physical and medical point of view, there are many fears that begin to haunt us. Let's examine the most critical.

"I don't think that I can stand the pain." Part of this comes from the "big boys don't cry" syndrome. It afflicts men much more than women. Underlying, however, is also the desire to maintain our composure and dignity under all circumstances. Let me share with you a few things that you will discover. Pain is relative. If you have had no pain and stub your toe in the night, it is catastrophic. If you have just recovered from a hemorrhoidectomy and stub your toe, you won't even wince. The majority of the pain we suffer is still mental, in response to the signal which the body sends to the brain. Many of our friends from the Middle and Far East have long since discovered the ability to minimize or to ignore pain. The attitude of the mind has much to do with how much potential suffering there is.

Don't get too far ahead of the process. This is another way of saying, "Don't borrow trouble until it comes." Dwight L. Moody, the lay evangelist at the turn of the century, was asked if he had the courage to be a martyr. He replied "Of course not. But if God desires me to be a martyr, He is perfectly capable of giving me the courage to fulfill the role when the time comes." When the proper time arrives, there will be much interior help if you need it. Medical science, however, doesn't want you to be a martyr. The discipline of pain control for terminal patients is an ever growing field. You will have all the help you need.

"I am afraid of the actual death process." Death represents the unknown and should be a matter of grave concern for us. Since we have not experienced death previously why shouldn't we be apprehensive? But hear this truth: you will never consciously experience death. Through either the administration of drugs or the body's own natural anesthesia (known as the comatose state) you will be asleep when it happens. Having been present through the years, I can assure you that it is almost identical to surgery. The patient never experiences surgery where there is a general anesthetic. Those around the table sometimes watch a very disturbing process. In fact it takes a strong stomach or professional dedication to survive it. But the patient has no such recollection or experience. He only experiences the effects of the surgery which in the long run are quite beneficial. So with death. It is not always easy for those who stand hour upon hour by the bedside and wait for the inevitable. But what they see, feel, and relate to is far different from that of the patient.

Death is not the enemy. Most of the time when it comes, it is welcomed by the patient and those loved ones who have been in the process. It is a friend that releases the body from turmoil, distortion and conflict. Death is a freeing from the limitations of disease and discomfort. It is a very real gift of God. Did you know that the Christian Church always remembers the saints of the day of their death? It is recognized as their most important birthday. Early Christians were considered psychotic. They were the first group in the history of man that went to the funeral singing hymns of joy and thanksgiving. It was a time of triumph for the loved one and not an hour of bleak despair. If all the promises of God are to be fulfilled, then it is to be at that time.

"But I feel so alone. No one can help me." From the time of your birth, you were never less alone. More people are thinking about you, praying for you, trying to find ways to convey love and support, working for your comfort than you can imagine. Your importance to a large number of people has become evident. It's not that you weren't important before. There was simply no reason to

38

emphasize it, and now there is. Your greatest temptation will be to withdraw from the people and shut off their opportunity to be part of your life and this experience.

You are not alone within either. God does not require our consciousness of His presence in order to minister to us, any more than a new-born infant has to be aware of the mother, in order to receive her gracious care. The first person whom I presented for confirmation in my first parish experienced death through cancer. She was a very lovely matron. Hers was a debilitating type of disease, and it produced several months in bed. Once in a mood of slight depression, she asked if I thought that God really cared. Though her background was anti-Catholic, the next visit I brought her a crucifix. I suggested that everytime she wondered, she was to look at God the Son on the cross. Thereafter, the crucifix was seldom absent from her hand. He not only knows and cares, but has been there ahead of us. We can never suffer as much as He suffered, humanly speaking. Through prayer we discover that He not only knows and cares, but is actually going through the experience with us. You will find Him present in the darkness of the night when you feel the most alone.

"But I have no time left." This is one of the side benefits of cancer. Unlike a mortal heart attack, or a stroke, we do have time and most of our abilities are undimmed. My thanksgiving is overflowing for this past year since my original surgery. So much has been accomplished, experienced, enjoyed. In some ways, it has been better than all the other years put together. I was also able to put down exactly what I felt I needed to do to have peace of mind at the time of death. The vast majority of these things have been accomplished and in the weeks that remain the list will almost be completed. I firmly believe that there is time to do everything that really must be done. But there is no time to waste in self-pity, or bemoaning the loss of time.

It does make you sort out your priorities. Much of the inanity and the foolishness of contemporary society will have to be immediately dropped with no apology. This can be the most productive time that you have ever experienced. You will discover the easing of other pressures. People understand that your life has to be your own and they will be both helpful and cooperative.

There is a marvelous club for cancer patients called One Day At A Time. The title tells the basic philosophy of the club. It is as close to living reality as is possible. You have never been guaranteed more than one day in your life. Today is that day. How can you make the most of it, from the time you awaken and give thanks, till you close your eyes in thanksgiving at the end? Fill it doing the things that are important to you. Enjoy the people that have been placed around you. Share the richness of what you have and are with them and you will discover that you have all the time in the world.

Terminal Illness
and Its Beneficial By-Products

How in the world could any good come from terminal illness? The terrible words themselves denote pain, suffering, deprivation, and defeat. Nor do we want any dear sweet person, in near perfect health, in a Mary Poppins voice, to tell us "But you must look on the bright side." This short chapter will be the most difficult to accept. I wouldn't dare write it except that I have really experienced it. And for those of you facing terminal illness who are open, the story wouldn't be complete without it.

Some of us have been privileged from early existence to see life as a fantastic adventure. Each day has been bursting with possibilities. We are constantly delighted and shocked by the things that happen, the doors that open, the opportunities that lie partially hidden all about us. We have refused to be locked in the box of anyone else's imagery or model. The idea of playing it safe is abhorrent to our embracing of existence. Life is to be experienced in its fullness, with all the enthusiasm and zest that the emotions can convey.

If we have lived this way, it doesn't matter what the experience is, we are going to drink from it fully, try to fathom all of its secrets, and be nourished by any goodness that can be extracted from it.

I guess the most important by-product of terminal illness is learning to accept the privilege of receiving. For many persons, giving is sheer delight and receiving is nearly impossible. There are many reasons why individuals cannot receive from others. Giving makes one feel superior, while receiving makes some persons feel inferior. With receiving there is the sense of obligation. Somehow, we must do for them at least as much as they have done for us. We would rather that they be indebted to us than vice versa. Receiving ties us to the giver and we would rather stand alone. If we receive we can hardly say, "I did it all myself."

When you are critically ill you instantly learn how to receive, and all the psychological defenses melt rapidly away. You control almost none of the factors. At times you are a fully dependent being, in the same way that you were in infancy. How you feel emotionally and physically is directed by the ministry of others. There is no way to fight it. The only chance you have is to cooperate with it. To your amazement, you begin to enjoy it. This is very central to a fulfilled life and if you had left this world through a heart attack, you would never have discovered it.

The receiving begins with the expression of loving concern from so many. There are the cards, letters, and phone calls. Why would any aside from your mother take the time to go out and shop for a card, and write a message and mail it to you? Astounding, but they do, because they really care. You would also be awed if you knew how many persons are praying for you, a vast number whom you don't even know. It matters little whether or not you believe in the efficacy of prayer. These people believe in it. And they believe in you, and your worth and value. And everyday, literally almost throughout the world, at all the different moments, persons are offering their prayers for your well-being.

From your family and close friends you are going to be receiving very direct acts of love and support, even if the family is one where "we never show our emotions". You are going to see very open expressions of love through emotion. My two sons and I have had the usual masculine standoff on emotional expression. Our greeting is a word and nod of the head. If it is a moment heavy with interpersonal exchange we may even shake hands. But two days after surgery I opened my eyes and my big twenty-year-old son was sitting, holding my hand, which he did for the next hour, and there was no embarrassment. He was meeting my need for loving physical support, from the fullness of his own heart. At that moment our relationship entered a new phase of understanding and expressiveness.

A few nights later, both sons (who were there daily and assisting a bit with the nursing care) asked if it wouldn't feel good to have a shampoo. Then they had to use engineering skills to determine a way that this could be done without disturbing my prone position. The tools at hand were limited but they got it accomplished. As they performed their task of love, I thought of each one, when as infants they laid in the baby bath, and were soaped, scrubbed and powdered. Our positions had finally reversed. At that moment I was no longer autocratic daddy. I was learning to receive. It was the same experience with my daughter some forty-five hundred miles away who through regular telephone calls and constant cards and letters gave her strength to her father in his weakness.

When I left the hospital, I sent a note to the superintendent of nurses congratulating her on her staff and singling out a couple of nurses for a Legion of Merit award. There was the one who had worked half the night packing me in ice. And the other who took care of me magnificently, and told me off regularly. She would have rather seen me stricken with bubonic plague than to have allowed five seconds of self-pity. At one point I would have gladly strangled her, if I had had enough strength to get out of bed, and could have become disengaged from the tubes. And every act and every word on her part was because she cared. The doctors each day brought more than medical direction. They brought obvious personal concern. They were in this thing with me, and doing all that was humanly possible. There isn't enough money in the world to repay dedicated medical professionals for their day and night ministration. From them I learned to receive.

In the more serious moments of the illness itself, there is time for inner quiet. At first this may sound like a very dubious benefit. Man fears silence and flees from it at every opportunity. There are those who suggest that he is really fleeing from himself. In the silence you come face to face with yourself.

Most of each day is spent in response to telephone, TV, spouse, children, boss, dog, and a host of responsibilities. The emotional energy starts to drain out when the alarm goes off, and continues unabated until we fall exhausted into bed at night. The power of recreative silence is never discovered. The chance to be "oneself" for a few minutes slips by unused. We are the servant, and at the command of all persons and incidents that pass by. After reading a biography of Marilyn Monroe, my instant reaction was, "It isn't a shame that she died. The tragedy is that she never lived." There was no time that was hers. There was no life that wasn't a reflection of the needs and desires of those about her. This wasn't unique to Miss Monroe. She shares it with a vast number of persons living today whose lives are not in the spotlight.

In terminal illness, your relationship to all others has drastically changed. "Business as usual" is no more. Most will be hypersensitive to your desires, and willing to back off and let you have both space and time. During the convalescent or final period, others are meeting your elemental needs of food, grooming, medicine, and anything else that comes to mind. You are free to let the mind emerge, to hear interior goodness and beauty, to feel all the muscles relax and the tension dissolve. At last you can be *you*. Whether in the vast movements of outer space or in Phillips Brooks' writing "How silently, how silently, the wondrous gift is given," the great creative powers of the universe seem to move most wondrously in the silences. This is a rare gift.

Another by-product is the chance to get things in perspective. Unique is the person whose time expenditure matches his value system. Most of us pour out our time and energy on those who cry the loudest. When you discover the shortness of time, there is an automatic examining of priorities. When John Wesley, the founder of Methodism, was asked what he would do if he knew that he would die in one week, he opened his appointment book to what he had already scheduled. However, most of us would act in a manner similar to that in an incident purported to have happened on a major university campus. An outstanding scientific lecturer was brought in for one evening. The lecture was open to the public. It was a brilliant oral dissertation, revealing the world as an integrated whole, and all things properly balanced in relationship to each other. When he completed his lecture there was supposed to be a question and answer session. However, his erudition was such that this university audience was stunned. Finally, one elderly man, who looked a bit down on his luck, held up his hand. The lecturer asked for his question. The old man said, "What if it's just the opposite?" Confused, the lecturer asked what he meant. The old man replied that he didn't know what he meant. But as he listened, it all sounded so good and so perfect, and he just got to wondering, "What if it's all just the opposite?" This will be the experience of many of us. We realize that all we have been taught in terms of value may be just the opposite. Whether for a few weeks or a few months, to live and do according to what we think is important is deeply satisfying and fulfilling. It is a rare gift that comes to few, except through this experience. You, who bear the stigma, are much blessed.

While you will discover many other beneficial by-products on your own, I would like to mention one other. It is the privilege of planning the completion of that which is important to you. In effect each of us has a time bank account. We go on spending day by day without a clue as to how much is left. For many, by accident or sudden organic failure, the account runs out without warning. For us, through the knowledge of medical science, we are given a fairly accurate approximate balance. This allows us to spend out the account on those things we consider the most significant. What would you like to complete: a rose garden, a little book of meditation for the terminally ill, proper estate planning, a cherished trip, a room on the house, the reading of Shakespeare's works? Make your list. There is time. And give thanks for some of the privileges that go with terminal illness.

Death—
A Christian Perspective

So often Christianity to us is moralism, or a cultural identity, or a series of beautiful stories not unlike fairy tales, or endless sermons that speak totally of a world that doesn't exist for the average listener. Thus, when trauma comes, the Christian faith has little or no meaning. As I mentioned earlier, it is theory, rather than experiential truth. The historical facts behind the theory are quite startling in themselves.

The event which took place, producing the Christian cult, has no real parallel in the history of man. Many religions have had myths about a messiah form. But *this* "myth" was actually historically enfleshed. He was incarnate, and His drama was lived out in our midst and is verifiable. Those who dismiss Christianity casually have never taken the trouble to investigate the historic proofs. The life of Jesus, and the events which took place, are much more easily authenticated than the life and writings of Plato, Socrates, and Aristotle, who lived before He did. No one thinks to question their existence, actions or statements because there was nothing that extraordinary about them. Nor does the content of their life and work make any remarkable demands on us.

The resurrection, or survival through death, is the key to the Christian movement. Without it, there would be no Christian Church, no New Testament. The movement apparently ended with the crucifixion of Jesus. His followers scattered, frightened for their lives. It was over. Only one event could have brought them back together again. Only one event could have so totally transformed their lives that ten of the twelve walked into death without hesitancy. How many persons do you know who will die for something that they know is blatantly untrue? Can you get a whole club of fiercely independent, argumentative day laborers to do it? The record is plain. The driving force of the Christian faith from day one was the resurrection and the experience of the apostles in seeing Jesus alive following death. The Christian concept of death, so well stated by Paul in his writing to the people in Corinth, had no historical antecedents. It was not theory. They had seen, touched, heard, smelled and tasted. This had happened not to a little esoteric group who pledged to tell the story. It happened over a period of time to larger and larger groups of persons, both followers and nonfollowers.

The death practices of Christians were basically unknown in prior periods and different religions. It all had a new base, and the base wasn't pious speculation. Christ's words gave the assurance that what had happened to Him would also happen to them. Death was not to be feared or even treated with awe. It was another birth process. As Paul said, "If God has provided a body for us here, He is perfectly capable of providing a body for us in the next life that will be in keeping with the demands of that existence." Practicing Christians of each generation have echoed the same basic sentiment. How can they be so sure when they are so far removed time-wise from the *Event*? The secret is that they really aren't. They have experienced Jesus as alive, as real and as substantial as did the Apostles. They have had communication, especially in love, that is light-years beyond autosuggestion.

To their agnostic friend they would say,

"I am sympathetic with where you are coming from. But never make the mistake of denying the truth of another's experience. It is sufficient to say, 'It is not true for me because I have not experienced it.' Otherwise, you close the door within you, and make it impossible for the growth of that experience to happen to you."

Besides the Christian sense of knowledge rather than belief in regard to life after death, philosophy has long sought to postulate possibilities. These are not arguments, but longings. And yet they are predicated on as much logic and rationality as those who vehemently deny the continuance of existence beyond death as a result of scientific theories.

They begin with the basic principle of life within the universe itself. Albert Einstein was doing fabulous work in the field just prior to his death. His statements would indicate that he had come from agnosticism into a position of theism in his latter years. Much of his understanding was based on the fact that while the universe may be expanding, nothing seems to escape it. The basic essentials in the universe change form, but nothing, nothing is actually ever destroyed. It reminds one of Alfred North Whitehead's statement of God in whom there is a "tender care that nothing be lost." If this is true of the material aspects of the universe, does it make sense that it would not be true of the highest form of life known, the spirit of man?

As we move into the realm of man, we cannot help but be awed, and especially at the humble beginnings of man. To sit one evening and listen to the works of a master, played by those who seemingly are possessed with something akin to perfect skill, is truly other-worldly. To stand in front of a canvas, painted by an artist who can portray life so vividly that it is fully conveyed with these inanimate objects, can almost reduce one to tears. To read the writings of those whose minds and spirits soared to places that most of us could never reach can place us in reverie. Is all of this ability, all of this insight, all of this humanity perfected, to be consigned to a thoughtless oblivion, finally to be wiped out with the death of all of humanity on some cataclysmic day? There is much that speaks to us of continued existence, far beyond the very short journey that is ours here. When Helen Keller was first told about Jesus, she said "I knew there had to be somebody like that." For many who have not had the privilege of a positive faith, the experience beyond death will provide a smile, and the comment "I knew there had to be something like this."

When Dr. Kübler-Ross' books began to

be published as well as the volume *Life after Life*, I could nod sagely as one who had been at the same place for many years. You cannot go into the death experience with hundreds, as I have, and not make some observations. These have no scientific validity. They are, in fact, beyond the realm of science. The startling quality, however, is their commonality. The pattern is remarkably similar to Christian and non-Christian, to believer and nonbeliever. God, evidently, has not an ounce of discrimination.

Let me simply recount two incidents that I personally observed. Having had the privilege of being there, they are truth to me. They can only be hearsay or theory to you. Almost always in the last hours the persons with whom I have stayed have been outwardly unconscious. Once there was a rare exception. Death would result from an inoperable aneurism, and the person I was counseling would suffer an internal hemorrhage. Otherwise, besides being weak, the individual was perfectly normal and healthy. We had had a chance to talk at length about the death experience and that which would happen beyond. If not anticipation, there seemed to be quietness and peace. The doctor had said the signs indicated it probably would not go beyond the day. In the afternoon, we were sitting and visiting very quietly. The parishioner was speaking as lucidly and rationally as always, with much ease. In the midst of talking to me she turned and spoke to "Mary." The only thing unusual was that she and I were alone in the room. This was repeated with "John" on the other side of the room. Then she continued her conversation with me. No drugs were being administered, and everything else was both normal and rational. A short time later, she closed her eyes and death ensued almost instantly.

At a proper time, I spoke to her daughter about the incident. She was quiet and thoughtful. She then explained that "Mary" and "John" were her mother's brother and sister. The three had been extremely close emotionally. The two had preceded her in death by several years. I could give all kinds of explanation of possibilities, psychological and otherwise. But having been a part of the actual experience, in honesty I would know that these explanations were untrue.

One other experience will suffice and it bears the traditional profile of countless others who had been considered dead from a medical point of view and then returned.

I was at the hospital, sitting with a couple, while the mother was undergoing surgery. The daughter told me that the mother had delayed the surgery as long as possible due to an abnormal fear of death. After three and a half hours, the surgeon came out and he was obviously concerned. Though the surgery seemed to have been successfully completed, the mother was in critical condition. He suggested that she had evidently gone into surgical shock and they were doing everything that could be done. He was not hopeful, however. With their permission he was asking the counsel of another urological surgeon. I began to try to prepare the couple for the mother's death which I expected would be announced within the hour.

A very short time later, the doctor came, with the consultant, and said that the life signs were diminishing and they had decided on further surgery. Her chances were slim to survive the surgery, but they were nonexistent otherwise. The couple agreed. Forty-five minutes later, the second surgeon came out, gowned and with mask dropped down. His forehead gave evidence of heavy perspiration. I knew what it meant.

He asked me if the woman was an Episcopalian. I replied "No, but it really doesn't matter." Then he turned to the couple and said "I'm sorry, but the body seemingly could not stand further injury. There has been heart failure. We have worked for some time for restoration to no avail. I'm afraid she has gone." He then turned back to me and said "Father, if you want to administer last rites, follow me." When we entered surgery, the body was lying on the table and all tubes had been removed. The surgical team was standing over in the corner quietly talking. The surgeon and I went to the body. He stood on one side and I on the other. Also being an Episcopalian, he responded in terms of the prayers. For the only time in such a position, I had an absolute compulsion to pray for her recovery. It wasn't as if the prayers would effect the recovery, but I felt she was going to recover and we were to pray for her needed strength. Feeling totally foolish I began such prayer. Before it was completed I heard a feminine voice proclaim loudly, "I think she moved." Within seconds the surgical team was back at the table, tubes reestablished, pumps working and I returned to the couple outside. All I said was, "The life signs have returned, but don't get your hopes up. She is terribly critical and if she recovers we could face the spectre of brain damage. But if perchance she does recover, I think it would be best that this never be mentioned to her. Now let's say our prayers for her." After surgery, in talking with the doctor, he said that he had not had an experience quite like it. He also suggested that due to the physical trauma, nothing should be said to her.

Her recovery was normal and I visited her each day in the hospital. We became friends. She went home and weeks passed. One day she appeared at my study door. She had come for a visit. She looked at my face a long time as if trying to read me; then she asked quietly, "Did I die during the surgery?" My immediate reaction was that the surgeon or her children had talked to her. So I asked "To whom have you been talking?" She said very openly, "No one." I responded "Then, what would make you think a thing like that?" She began to share a very vivid recollection. She recalled the beginning of the administration of the anesthetic and then nothing. Suddenly, she began to hear the most exalted, rich, and fulfilling music. It was as if she had perfect pitch and could savor each note of each instrument, and yet the harmonious quality was perfection. She said that it seemed her emotions, which were lifted to an ecstatic level could hardly bear the excitement of it. Then came colors, again so deep and rich, as to beggar man's ability to describe. Finally, there was a light and it appeared to be coming through a tunnel. The light didn't hurt her eyes and she peered into it. From the light and tunnel there emerged the figure of her husband. He had preceded her in death by several years. She said that he looked wonderful, and, smiling, he walked toward her. As he drew very near, she held out her hand to him. With total kindness and concern appearing on his face, he slowly shook his head. While no words were heard, she had the distinct feeling that he was saying "Not yet." He turned and walked back into the tunnel. And there was no further memory.

When she finished her very intense narration, she again asked "Father Conley, did I die during surgery?" Hers was a classic statement of the experience of those who have apparently died and then been restored. And as is true in most cases, she lost all fear of death and it was a life-changing experience. In later years she had surgery again but, oh, so differently. She has since experienced death, and this time they went back through the tunnel hand in hand.

By itself, this little incident would have small meaning. Again, it can be so easily explained by hallucination, drug response, projection. But it does not stand alone. It is the obvious common occurrence and so dramatic that the unconscious memory reproduces it to the conscious mind.

For the person of any religious faith, who has had personal experience of the love of God, all explanations and all illustrations are needless and redundant. If God does indeed exist, and His nature is love, then there is no further question. The first scripture learned by the little child has the total meaning. "God so loved the world that He gave His only begotten Son, that whosoever believes in Him should not perish, but have eternal life."

A Final Word

At this moment I don't know whether two months, five weeks, or eight days remain. The destructive effects are felt in my body, but more as minor aches and pains. There is no depression and no apprehension. Life is life. And once you begin to really experience it, nothing can diminish it. And there won't be any final word because that isn't true to life. "In the beginning was the Word . . . as it was in the beginning, is now, and ever shall be, world without end." Life always continues to expand, to open doors, to offer great promises. But we have to complete each course, before we are eligible for the next.

As death approaches for most there is a heroic desire to rise to the occasion, to be in command, to cope until the weakness of the flesh allows only passive resistance. It is typified by one of the final scenes of the award winning movie "Rocky". The young tank fighter has been given a chance to fight the world champion. He responds with such training, commitment and intensity of desire, that you almost join him in believing that the miracle can happen. The night before the fight, at the height of his fervor, he goes to the empty arena and meditates on the event to come. In the middle of the night as he returns to his drab apartment, his girl friend awakens and asks him "What's wrong?" Facing the trauma of reality, he says quietly, "I can't win." She responds by asking, "What are we going to do?" With the total depth of his being he responds—"No one has ever gone the distance with him. If I can just be on my feet when the final bell sounds, it will be all right." It was a plea for an inner victory, based on human dignity and courage. This speaks eloquently for the response of the person facing the immediate experience of death. With the help of capable medical assistance, dedicated to the true well-being of the patient, this is a reasonable goal.

There is a beautiful collect in the Book of Common Prayer. It prays that as the body

fails, even so may the soul of man grow.
There is so much truth embodied here. But it
is not automatic. "Seek and you will find" is a
cardinal truth of life. So very little happens by
accident. You have to know what you want to
have happen. The body has received much
attention and care from you and has probably
served you well. Now, you can turn it over to
the others. Ignore it as much as possible, and
concentrate on the inner you. Instead of fight-
ing to find life, let life find you. Now is the
time for the inner quiet, the non-struggle, the
expectant passivity. You will experience the
work of the Holy Spirit, as the mystics have
known through the centuries. Growth will
come unheralded. Your vision, your understanding, your insight will enlarge. You will
find within, the peace that passes understanding.

In his early eighties, Benjamin Franklin
was taking his customary walk on the streets
of Philadelphia. A young admirer greeted him
with the question. "And how is Mr. Franklin
today?" The old gentleman responded, "Well,
the house in which he lives is in a growing
state of disrepair. The roof is thin, you can
hardly see out of the windows, the boards
creak, and it has become a bit cold and drafty.
It is apparent that he will have to leave the

house before long. But, Mr. Franklin is very well, thank you."

For some there will be speculation about the next life. No one here knows. If someone did, we could not comprehend his description. It would be like trying to explain this life to an infant in the womb. What would color, food, music, mean to one with such limited existence, who had never experienced these glories? And after your explanation, would the infant want to leave the security of the present environment for this new venture? Hardly! But fortunately there is no choice. The day and the hour arrive, and the child is ushered (sometimes protesting) into this present world. The only thing we do know for certain is that it will be entirely different than we expect. Fr. Homer Rogers has a delightful story. Two men died. One was a pillar of the Episcopal Church, the key man of the diocese, the bishop's right hand man, always wheeling, dealing, and organizing. His death was celebrated by a Solemn Pontifical Requiem Mass in the jam-packed cathedral. And the eulogy placed him very close to Saints Peter and Paul. That's what the people saw. The man went through the experience of death and was suddenly confronted in the next life by a vast number of people offering their love

68

and adoration to God in Eucharistic fashion. And he said, "Oh hell, the same old thing." And for him, hell it was. The other man was a professor. He hadn't had a great deal of contact with organized religion. So much seemed unreal and was almost contradictory to that which was professed. He was ignored by the Church as an unconvertible agnostic. His life had been dedicated to the pursuit of truth for the well-being of man, regardless of where it took him. In honesty and humility, he gave himself to each day, and to those about him. At his death, only the family and a handful of friends gathered at the grave. A simple prayer by a layman was offered. That is what the people saw. But following death the professor was suddenly face to face with God, and saw there the fullness of Truth as he had always sought. And he said "Well, I'll be damned!" But he wasn't. He was saved.

As we move into the experience, in child-like trust we say, "I may not know *what's* there. But I know *who's* there." The God of sacrificing love, the God of Jesus Christ, can be trusted with that which He has created, with that which He has protected and in so many ways really redeemed. Paul was not just rhapsodizing when he said "Eye has not seen, nor ear heard, the wonderful things which God has prepared for those who love Him."

This little scenario is enacted every evening on the quiet beaches in the islands of my beloved Hawaii. The child has been playing happily, making sand castles and cities and roads. In the sheer fun of it, there has been no awareness that the sun is setting and the cool evening breezes are beginning to blow. Suddenly, the child looks up and there is father smiling and saying, "Come, it is time to go." The child gets up, dusts off, and we see them walking hand in hand to the comfort of home and the evening meal prepared.

I once said to the cathedral congregation "One day you will hear that I have experienced death. If you listen closely, you will hear the peal of Irish laughter, as I go forth to life's greatest adventure." The time is near. And I salute you, my fellow traveler, in the Way.